POCKET BEATLES
FOR GUITAR

Edited by Milton Okun

ISBN: 0-89524-126-9

Exclusively Distributed By

Cherry
Lane
Music
Co., inc.

P.O. BOX 4247•GREENWICH, CT. 06830

Contents

Across The Universe

Words and Music by
JOHN LENNON & PAUL McCARTNEY

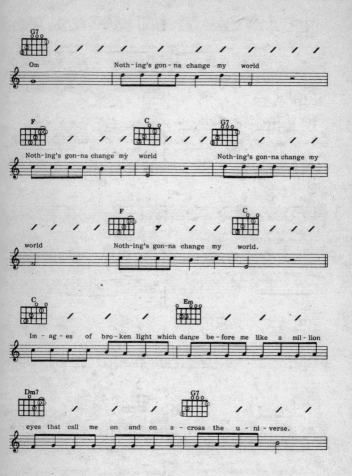

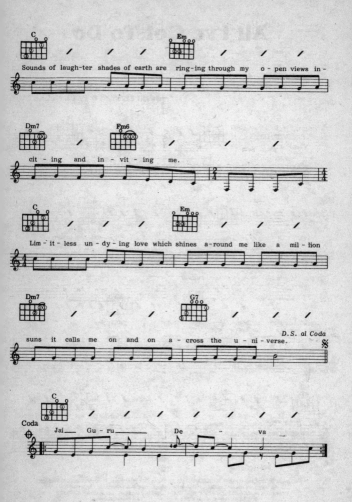

Sounds of laugh-ter shades of earth are ring-ing through my o - pen views in-cit-ing and in - vit - ing me. Lim - it - less un-dy - ing love which shines a-round me like a mil - lion suns it calls me on and on a - cross the u - ni - verse.

D.S. al Coda

Coda

Jai_ Gu - ru_ De - va

All I've Got To Do

Words and Music by
JOHN LENNON & PAUL McCARTNEY

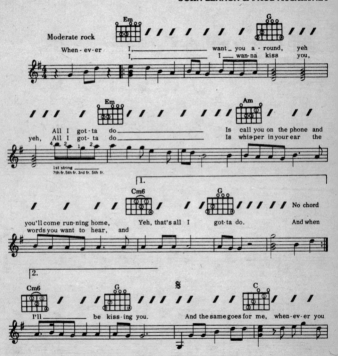

want me at all. I'll be here, yes, I will. When‑ev‑er you can, you

just got‑ta call on me, __ yeh, __ you just got‑ta call on me.

last time end here No chord | And when I, _____ I __ wan‑na kiss you,

yeh, All I wan‑na do _____ Is call you on the phone and

you'll come run‑ning home yeh, that's all I got‑ta do. *Go back to* 𝄋

9

All My Loving

Starting note
for singing:

Words and Music by
JOHN LENNON & PAUL McCARTNEY

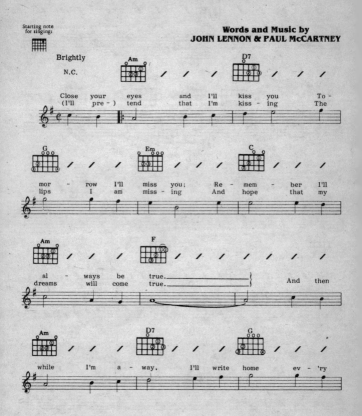

Brightly

N.C. | Am | D7

Close your eyes and I'll kiss you To-
(I'll pre-) tend that I'm kiss-ing The

G | Em | C

mor - row I'll miss you; Re - mem - ber I'll
lips I am miss - ing And hope that my

Am | F

al - ways be true. And then
dreams will come true.

Am | D7 | G

while I'm a-way, I'll write home ev-'ry

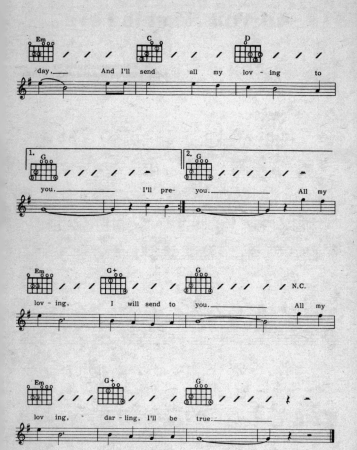

day,___ And I'll send all my lov - ing to

1. G
you._____ I'll pre - you._____ All my

2. G

Em   G+   G   N.C.
lov - ing, I will send to you._____ All my

Em   G+   G
lov ing, dar - ling, I'll be true._____

All You Need Is Love

Words and Music by
JOHN LENNON & PAUL McCARTNEY

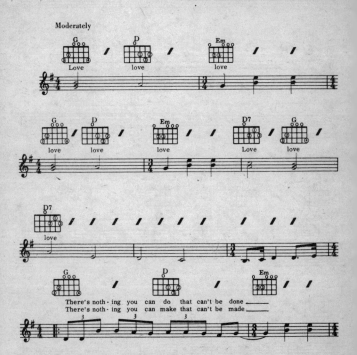

13

And I Love Her

**Words and Music by
JOHN LENNON & PAUL McCARTNEY**

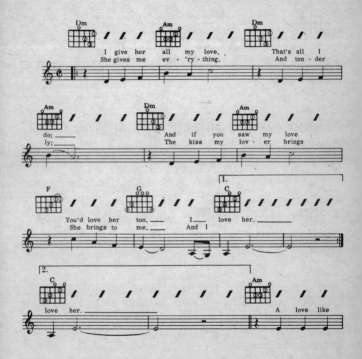

And Your Bird Can Sing

Words and Music by
JOHN LENNON & PAUL McCARTNEY

Moderately

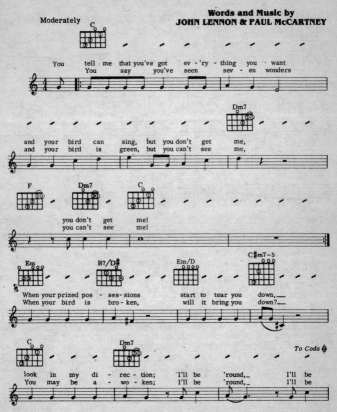

You tell me that you've got ev - 'ry - thing you want
You say you've seen sev - en wonders

and your bird can sing, but you don't get me,
and your bird is green, but you can't see me,

you don't get me!
you can't see me!

When your prized pos - ses - sions start to tear you down,
When your bird is bro - ken, will it bring you down?

look in my di - rec - tion; I'll be 'round,__ I'll be
You may be a - wo - ken; I'll be 'round,__ I'll be

To Coda ⊕

16

'round.

Dm7

G7   C   D. S. ½ al Coda ✇

Coda G7   C

'round.   You tell me that you've heard ev - 'ry

sound there is   and your bird can swing, but you can't hear

Dm7   F   Dm7   C

me,   you can't hear me!

Another Girl

Words and Music by
JOHN LENNON & PAUL McCARTNEY

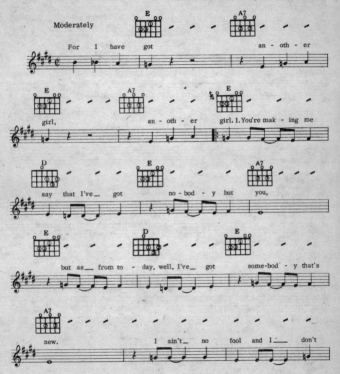

2. She's sweeter than all the girls, and I've met quite a few.
   Nobody in all the world can do what she can do.
   And so I'm tellin' you, this time you'd better stop.
   For I have got *(etc.)*

3. I don't wanna say that I've been unhappy with you,
   But as from today, well, I've seen somebody that's new.
   I ain't no fool and I don't take what I don't want.
   For I have got *(etc.)*

All Together Now

Starting note
for singing:

Moderato

**Words and Music by
JOHN LENNON & PAUL McCARTNEY**

One, two, three, four, Can I have a lit-tle more?
A, B, C, D, Can I bring my friend to tea?

Five, six, sev-en, eight, nine, ten,___ I love you,___
E, F, G, H, I, J,___ I love you,___

1. (hold)

2. ___ Bom bom bom Bom-pa bom, Sail the ship, Bom-pa bom,

Chop the tree, Bom-pa bom, Skip the rope, Bom-pa bom,

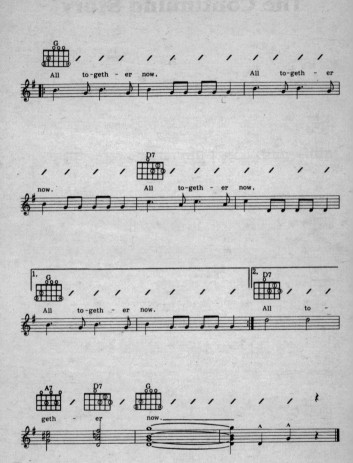

The Continuing Story Of Bungalow Bill

Words and Music by
JOHN LENNON & PAUL McCARTNEY

2. Deep in the jungle where the mighty tiger lies
   Bill and his elephants were taken by surprise,
   So Captain Marvel zapped him right between the eyes. All the children sing: (Chos)

3. The children asked him if to kill was not a sin,
   "Not when he looked so fierce," his mother butted in,
   If looks could kill it would have been us instead of him. All the children sing: (Chos)

Baby's In Black

Words and Music by
JOHN LENNON & PAUL McCARTNEY

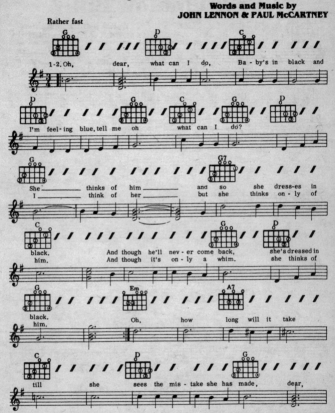

Baby You're A Rich Man

**Words and Music by
JOHN LENNON & PAUL McCARTNEY**

How of-ten have you been there, of-ten e-nough to know.
Tuned to a nat-ur-al E hap-py to be that way.

What did you see when you were there, noth-ing that does-n't show.
Now that you've found an-oth-er key, what are you going to play?

Ba-by, you're a rich man, Ba-by, you're a rich man, Ba-by, you're a rich man, too. You

keep all your mon-ey in a big brown bag in-side a zoo, what a thing to do!

Ba-by, you're a rich man, Ba-by, you're a rich man, Ba-by, you're a rich man, too. D.S. %

last time repeat last 4 bars and fade

27

Back In The U.S.S.R.

Words and Music by
JOHN LENNON & PAUL McCARTNEY

Modto.

Flew in from Mi - a - mi Beach, B. O. A. C., Did-n't get to bed last
night. On the way the pa-per bag was on my knee, Man, I had a dread-ful
flight. I'm back in the U.S. S. R., You don't know how lucky you are, boy,
Back in the U.S. S. R.,
Been a - way so long I hard - ly
Show me round your snow peaked moun - tains
knew the place, Gee, it's good to be back home.
way down South, take me to your dad-dy's farm.
Leave it till to - mor-row to un-
Let me hear your ba - la - lai - kas

No chord

pack my case Hon-ey, dis-con-nect the phone.
ring-ing out, Come and keep your com-rade warm. I'm back in the U. S. S. R.,

You don't know how luck-y you are, boy. Back in the U. S.,

back in the U. S., back in the U. S. S. R. Well, the

U-kraine girls real-ly knock me out, they leave the West be-hind. And

Mos-cow girls make me sing and shout _ that Georgia's al-ways on my mi - mi -

mi- mi- mi- mi- mi- mi- mi mind. Back in the U. S. S. R., Oh, yeah.

D.S. al Coda

29

The Ballad Of John And Yoko

Words and Music by
JOHN LENNON & PAUL McCARTNEY

Boogie - rock feeling

VERSE: Stand-ing in the dock at South-amp-ton, try'n to get to Hol-land or France, The man in the mac said you've got to go back you know they didn't ev-en give us a chance. Christ! You know it ain't eas-y, you know how hard it can be, The way things are go-ing they're going to cru-ci-fy me.

(Repeat for additional verses)

Bridge

Sav-ing up your mon-ey for a rain-y day, giv-ing all your clothes to cha-ri-

ty. Last night the wife said, oh boy, when you're dead you

don't take noth-ing with you but your soul, _____ Think!

(D.C. for more verses)

Additional Verses

2. Finally made the plane into Paris, honeymooning down the Seine,
   Peter Brown called to say, you can make it O.K.,
   You can get married in Gibraltar near Spain.
   Christ! You know it ain't easy, you know how hard it can be.
   The way things are going, they're going to crucify me.

3. Drove from Paris to the Amsterdam Hilton, talking in our beds for a week.
   The newspapers said, say what're you doing in bed,
   I said we're only trying to get us some peace. Christ! You know it ain't easy (etc.)

(Go to bridge)

4. Made a lightning trip to Vienna, eating choc'late cake in a bag.
   The newspapers said, she's gone to his head, they look just like two Gurus in drag.
   Christ, you know it ain't easy (etc.)

5. Caught the early plane back to London, fifty acorns tied in a sack.
   The men from the press said we wish you success, it's good to have the both of you back.
   Christ, you know it ain't easy (etc.)

Birthday

Words and Music by
JOHN LENNON & PAUL McCARTNEY

Fast

A7 / / / / / / / /

You say it's your birth-day,

/ / / / / / / /

D7

It's my birth-day, too, yeah.

They

/ / / / A7 / / / /

say it's your birth-day,

We're gon-na have a good time.

E7 / / / / A7 / / / /

I'm glad it's your birth-day,

Hap-py birth-day to you.

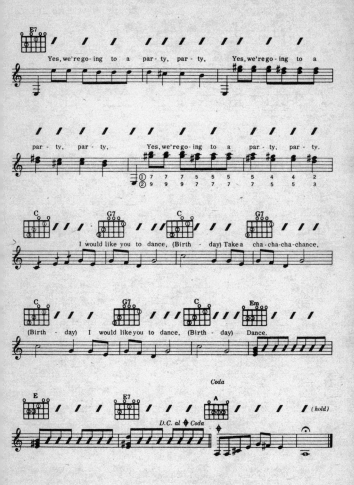

Blackbird

Words and Music by
JOHN LENNON & PAUL McCARTNEY

Moderately slow, in 2

34

Blue Jay Way

Words and Music by
GEORGE HARRISON

2. Well, it only goes to show, and I told them where to go.
   Ask a policeman on the street; There's so many there to meet.
   Please don't be long. (etc.)

3. Now it's past my bed I know, and I'd really like to go.
   Soon will be the break of day, sitting here in Blue Jay Way.
   Please don't be long. (etc.)

Can't Buy Me Love

Words and Music by
JOHN LENNON & PAUL McCARTNEY

I'll buy you a dia-mond ring, my friend if it makes you feel al-
I'll give you all I've got to give if you say you love me

right, I'll get you an-y-thing my friend, if it
too, I may not have a lot to give, but what I've

makes you feel al-right, } For I don't care too much for mon-ey, for
got I'll give to you, }

1. mon-ey can't buy me love. **2.** love. Can't buy me love,

Ev-'ry-bod-y tells me so, can't buy me love.

No no no   no   Say you don't need no dia - mond ring and I'll be sat - is - fied, Tell me that you want those kind of things   that mon - ey just can't buy,   I don't care too much for mon-ey,   for mon - ey can't buy me love. Can't buy me love,   love,   Can't buy me love.

(hold)

Come And Get It

Words and Music by
PAUL McCARTNEY

Starting note
for singing:

Moderately

If you want it here it is, come and get it; Mm _____ make your mind up _____ fast. If you want it an - y time I can give it, But you bet - ter hur - ry 'cos it may not _____

last.   Did I hear you say that there must be a catch?__

Will you walk a-way from a fool and his mon - ey?   If you

want it,   here it is, come and get it, But you bet - ter

hur-ry 'cos it's go-ing__ fast.   If you

fast.

Cry Baby Cry

Words and Music by
JOHN LENNON & PAUL McCARTNEY

Slowly, in 2

Cry, ba - by, cry; make your moth - er sigh. She's old e - nough to know bet - ter. 1. The King of Mar - i - gold was in the kitch - en cook - ing break - fast for the queen. The

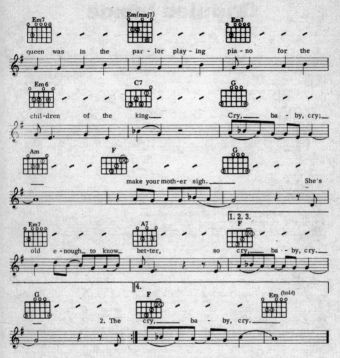

2. The king was in the garden picking flowers for a friend who came to play.
   The queen was in the playroom painting pictures for the children's holiday.
   Cry, baby, cry; *(etc.)*

3. The Duchess of Kircaldy always smiling and arriving late for tea.
   The duke was having problems with a message at the local Bird and Bee.
   Cry, baby, cry; *(etc.)*

4. At twelve o'clock a meeting 'round the table for a seance in the dark,
   With voices out of nowhere put on specially by the children for a lark.
   Cry, baby, cry; *(etc.)*

Crippled Inside

Words and Music by
JOHN LENNON

Starting note
for singing:

Moderate country ragtime, in 2 (♩ = 1 beat)

You can shine your shoes and wear a suit,
You can wear a mask and paint your face,

(hold C chord--) (Opt. fill)

You can comb your hair and look quite cute,
You can call your-self the hu-man race,

(hold F chord---)

You can hide your face be-hind a smile
You can wear a col-lar and a tie

(hold C chord--)

One thing you can't hide is when you're crip-pled in-

1. side. N.C.

2. side. Well, now you

know that your cat has nine lives, babe,

nine lives to it - self,___ But

you on - ly got one, and a dog's life ain't fun,

ma-ma, take a look___ out-side!_____

You can go to church and sing a hymn,   You can

judge me by the col-or of my skin,

You can live a lie till you die;

Twice as slow

One thing you can't hide___   is when you're crip-pled in-

side.

A Day In The Life

**Words and Music by
JOHN LENNON & PAUL McCARTNEY**

love to turn you _____ on. _____ No chords

I heard the news to-day, oh boy, Four thou-sand holes in Black-burn

Lan-ca-shire. And though the holes were ra-ther small,

They had to count them all, Now they know how man-y holes it takes to fill the Al-bert

Hall. _____ I'd love to turn _____ you _____ on. (hold)

Day Tripper

Words and Music by
JOHN LENNON & PAUL McCARTNEY

Starting note
for singing:

Moderate rock

1. Got a good rea - son   for tak - ing the eas - y way
2. She's a big teas - er,   she took me half   the way
3. Tried to please her,   she on - ly played one-night

out,   Got a good rea - son   for
there,   She's a big teas - er,
stands,   Tried to please   her,

tak - ing the eas - y way out now. She was a Day_____
she took me half___ the way there, now. She was a Day
she on - ly played_ one-night stands, now. She was a Day

48.

Dear Prudence

Words and Music by
JOHN LENNON & PAUL McCARTNEY

1. Dear   Pru - dence,   won't you come out to   play.
2. Dear   Pru - dence,   o - pen up   your   eyes.
3. Dear   Pru - dence,   let   me   see   you   smile.

Dear   Pru - dence,   greet a brand new   day.
Dear   Pru - dence,   see the sun - ny   skies.
Dear   Pru - dence,   like a lit - tle   child.

51

Dig It

**Words and Music by
JOHN LENNON, PAUL McCARTNEY,
GEORGE HARRISON & RICHARD STARKEY**

Don't Let Me Down

Words and Music by
JOHN LENNON & PAUL McCARTNEY

do me,   yes,   she does.
done me,   she done me good.
Don't let me down,

Don't let me down,____   don't let me down,____

don't let me down.____   I'm in love for the first time,

don't you know it's gon-na   last.   It's a love that lasts for-

ev - er,   it's a love that had no past.   *D.C. al ◆ Coda*   (hold)

No chords

◆ Coda

Dr. Robert

Words and Music by
JOHN LENNON & PAUL McCARTNEY

Moderately, in 2

2. If you're down he'll pick you up, Dr. Robert.
Take a drink from his special cup, Dr. Robert.
Dr. Robert.
He's a man you must believe, helping everyone in need.
No one can succeed like Dr. Robert.
Well, well, well, *(etc.)*

3. My friend works with the national health, Dr. Robert.
Don't pay money just to see yourself with Dr. Robert.
Dr. Robert.
You're a new and better man. He helps you to understand.
He does everything he can, Dr. Robert.
Well, well, well, *(etc.)*

Drive My Car

Words and Music by
JOHN LENNON & PAUL McCARTNEY

Medium Rock beat

1. Asked a girl what she want-ed to be.

She said, "Ba-by, can't you see?

I wan-na be fa-mous, a star of the screen, but

you can do some-thing in be-tween.

Ba-by, you can drive my car.

2. I told that girl that my prospects were good.
   She said, "Baby, it's understood.
   Working for peanuts is all very fine,
   But I can show you a better time.
   Baby, you can drive my car. *(etc.)*

3. I told that girl I could start right away.
   She said, "Baby, I've got something to say.
   I got no car and it's breaking my heart,
   But I've found a driver, that's a start.
   Baby, you can drive my car. *(etc.)*

Eight Days A Week

Words and Music by
JOHN LENNON & PAUL McCARTNEY

Moderato

1. Ooh, I need your love, babe, guess you know it's
2. 3. Love you ev-'ry day, girl, al-ways on my

true. Hope you need my love, babe,
mind. One thing I can say, girl,

just like I need you. Hold me,
love you all the time.

love me, hold me, love me,

ain't got noth-in' but love, babe,
ain't got noth-in' but love, girl, Eight days a

week. Eight days a week I

Fine

love you, Eight days a

week is not e-nough to show I care.

D.C. al Fine

Eleanor Rigby

Words and Music by
JOHN LENNON & PAUL McCARTNEY

in a jar by the door___ who is it for?___

All the lone-ly peo-ple, where do they all come from?

All the lone-ly peo-ple, where do they all be-long? *(Last time hold)*

Father McKenzie, writing the words of a sermon that no one will hear, no one comes near.

Look at him working, darning his socks in the night when there's nobody there, what does he care?

All the lonely people, where do they all come from?

All the lonely people, where do they all belong?

Eleanor Rigby, died in the church and was buried along with her name, nobody came.

Father McKenzie, wiping the dirt from his hands as he walks from the grave, no one was saved.

All the lonely people, where do they all come from?

All the lonely people, where do they all belong?

Every Little Thing

Words and Music by
JOHN LENNON & PAUL McCARTNEY

Moderate rock

1. When I'm walk-ing be - side her   Peo-ple tell me I'm
2. I re - mem-ber the first time   I was lone-ly with-

luck - y,   Yes, I know I'm a luck - y guy.
out her,   Yes, I'm think - ing a - bout her now.

3. Ev - 'ry lit - tle thing she does   she does for me,   yeah.

And you know the things she does   she does for me,   yeah.

Fixing A Hole

Words and Music by
JOHN LENNON & PAUL McCARTNEY

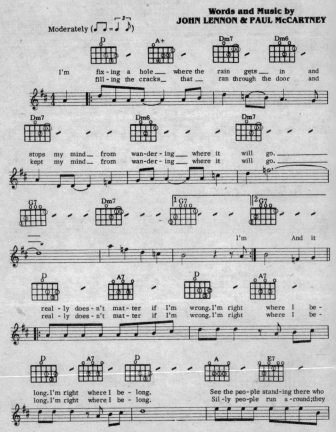

For No One

Words and Music by
JOHN LENNON & PAUL McCARTNEY

Starting note for singing:

Moderately

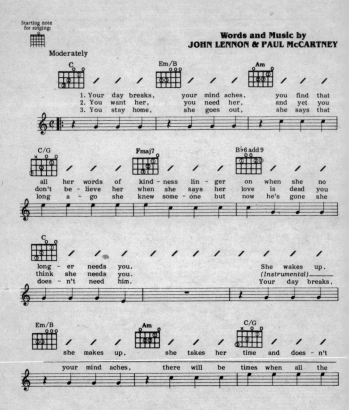

1. Your day breaks, your mind aches, you find that all her words of kind - ness lin - ger on when she no long - er needs you. She wakes up,
2. You want her, you need her, and yet you don't be - lieve her when she says her love is dead you think she needs you. (Instrumental)
3. You stay home, she goes out, she says that long a - go she knew some - one but now he's gone she does - n't need him. Your day breaks,

she makes up, she takes her time and does - n't your mind aches, there will be times when all the

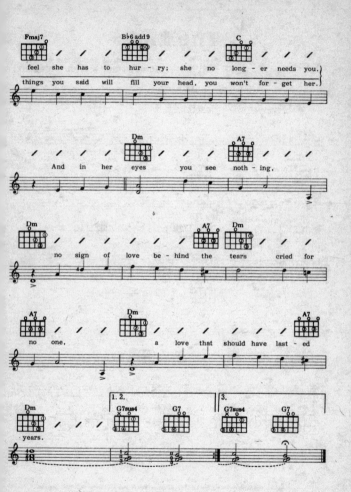

feel she has to hur-ry; she no long-er needs you.)
things you said will fill your head, you won't for-get her.

And in her eyes you see noth-ing,

no sign of love be-hind the tears cried for

no one, a love that should have last-ed

years.

The End

Words and Music by
JOHN LENNON & PAUL McCARTNEY

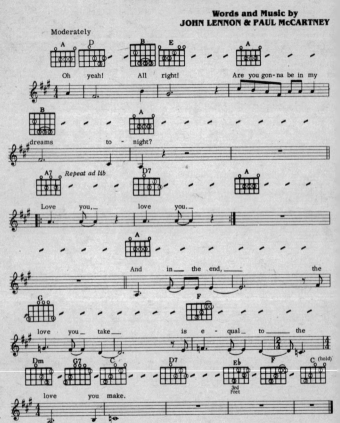

Get Back

Words and Music by
JOHN LENNON & PAUL McCARTNEY

Jo Jo was a man who thought he was a lon - er, But he knew it could - n't last. Jo Jo left his home in Tuc - son, Ar - i - zo - na, for some Cal - i - for - nia grass. Get back! Get back! Get back to where you once be - longed. Get back! Get back! Get back to where you once be - longed.

Sweet Loretta Modern thought she was a woman,
But she was another man.
All the girls around her said she's got it coming,
But she gets it while she can.

Get back! Get back!
Get back to where you once belonged.
Get back! Get back!
Get back to where you once belonged.

Girl

Words and Music by
JOHN LENNON & PAUL McCARTNEY

Give Peace A Chance

Words and Music by
JOHN LENNON & PAUL McCARTNEY

Moderately

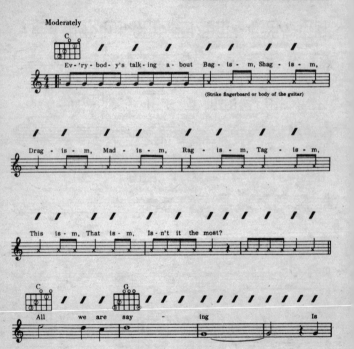

Ev-'ry-bod-y's talk-ing a-bout Bag - is - m, Shag - is - m,

(Strike fingerboard or body of the guitar)

Drag - is - m, Mad - is - m, Rag - is - m, Tag - is - m,

This is - m, That is - m, Is-n't it the most?

All we are say - ing Is

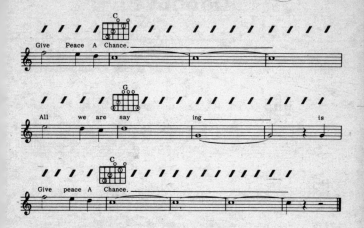

Give Peace A Chance. _____

All   we   are   say   ing _____   is

Give   peace A   Chance. _____

2. Ev'rybody's talking about
   Ministers, Sinisters, Banisters and Canisters,
   Bishops and Fishops, Rabbits and Popeyes,
   Bye-bye Bye-byes.

   All we are saying is Give Peace A Chance.
   All we are saying is Give Peace A Chance.

3. Let me tell you now,
   Ev'rybody's talking about
   Revolution, Evolution, Mastication, Flagellation,
   Regulations, Integregations, Meditation, United Nations,
   Congratulations.

   All we are saying is Give Peace A Chance.
   All we are saying is Give Peace A Chance.

4. Oh, let's stick to it,
   Ev'rybody's talking about
   John and Yoko, Timmy Leary, Rosemary, Tommy Smothers,
   Bobby Dylan, Tommy Cooper, Derek Taylor, Norman Mailer,
   Alan Ginsberg, Hare Krishna, Hare, Hare Krishna.

   All we are saying is Give Peace A Chance.
   All we are saying is Give Peace A Chance.
   All we are saying is Give Peace A Chance.
   All we are saying is Give Peace A Chance.

Goodbye

Starting note
for singing:

Words and Music by
JOHN LENNON & PAUL McCARTNEY

Moderately bright

1. Please don't wake me up too late, to-
2. Songs that lin-gered on my lips to ex-
3. Far a-way my lov-er sings a

mor - row comes____ and I will
cite me now____ and lin - ger
lone - ly song____ and calls me

not be late.____
on be my mind.____
to his side.____

Late to - day when it be - comes to-
Leave your flow - ers at my door, I'll
When a song of lone - ly love in -

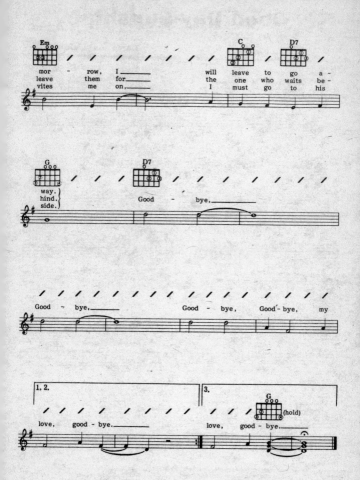

Em

mor - row, I
leave them for
vites me on,

will the
I must go

C

leave to
one who
go waits

D7

go a -
to be -
to his

G

way.
hind.
side.

D7

Good - bye,

Good - bye,

Good - bye, Good - bye, my

1. 2.

love, good - bye.

3.

G (hold)

love, good - bye.

Good Day Sunshine

Words and Music by
JOHN LENNON & PAUL McCARTNEY

VERSE 2

We take a walk the sun is shin-ing down, burns my feet as they touch the ground.

Solo

Repeat Chorus

VERSE 3 And then we lie be-neath a shad-y tree,

I love her and she lov-ing me.__ She feels good she knows she's look-ing fine, I'm so proud to know that she is mine.

Repeat Chorus and fade

Got To Get You Into My Life

Starting note
for singing:

Words and Music by
JOHN LENNON & PAUL McCARTNEY

tell you I need you ev-'ry sin-gle day of my
want you to hear me say, we'll be to-gether ev-'ry
tell you I need you ev-'ry sin-gle day of my

life.
day.
life?

Got to get you in-to my life!

D.C. al Coda

Coda (hold)

A Hard Day's Night

Words and Music by
JOHN LENNON & PAUL McCARTNEY

Hello, Goodbye

Words and Music by
JOHN LENNON & PAUL McCARTNEY

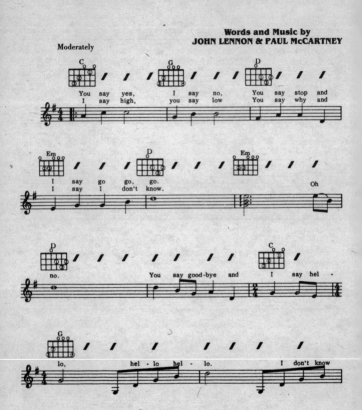

Hello Little Girl

Words and Music by
JOHN LENNON & PAUL McCARTNEY

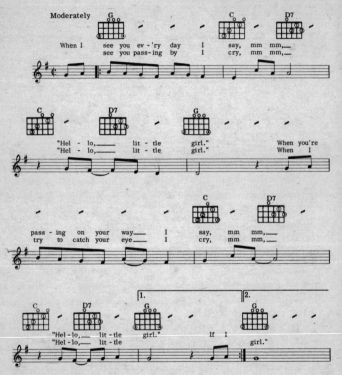

Help!

Words and Music by
JOHN LENNON & PAUL McCARTNEY

Now I find I've changed my mind, I've o- pened up the doors.
I know that I just need you like I've nev- er done be- fore.

Help me if you can, I'm feel-ing down _____ And I

do ap-pre-ci- ate you be-ing 'round. _____ Help me get my

feet back on the ground. _____ Won't you please, please help __

me? _____ please help __ me? Help me! Help me! __ oo.

Here There And Everywhere

Words and Music by
JOHN LENNON & PAUL McCARTNEY

Moderately slow

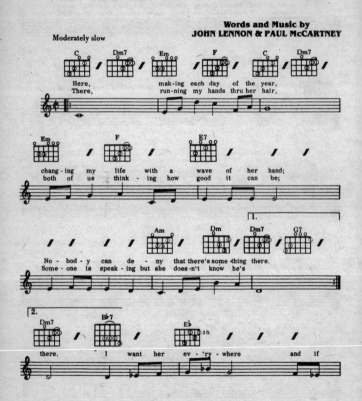

Here,
There,

mak-ing each day of the year,
run-ning my hands thru her hair,

chang-ing my life with a wave of her hand;
both of us think - ing how good it can be;

No - bod - y can de - ny that there's some-thing there.
Some - one is speak-ing but she does-n't know he's

there. I want her ev - 'ry - where and if

Hey Bulldog

Words and Music by
JOHN LENNON & PAUL McCARTNEY

Moderately

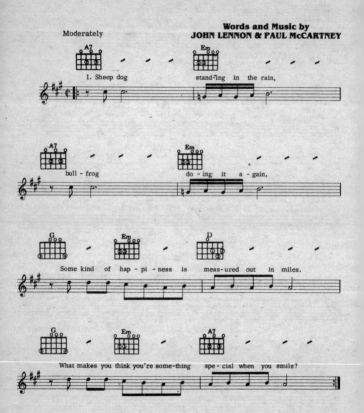

1. Sheep dog stand-ing in the rain, bull-frog do-ing it a-gain. Some kind of hap-pi-ness is meas-ured out in miles. What makes you think you're some-thing spe-cial when you smile?

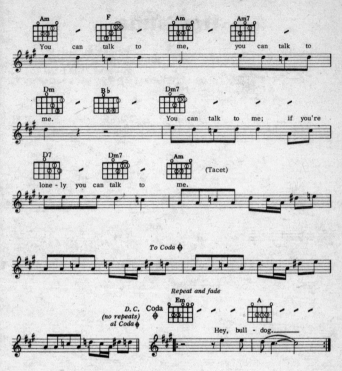

2. Childlike, no one understands;
   Jackknife in your sweaty hands.
   Some kind of innocence is measured out in years.
   You don't know what it's like to listen to your fears.
   You can talk to me, *(etc.)*

3. Big man walking in the park,
   Wigwam frightened of the dark.
   Some kind of solitude is measured out in you.
   You think you know it, but you haven't got a clue.
   You can talk to me, *(etc.)*

Hey Jude

Words and Music by
JOHN LENNON & PAUL McCARTNEY

Her Majesty

Words and Music by
JOHN LENNON & PAUL McCARTNEY

Bright

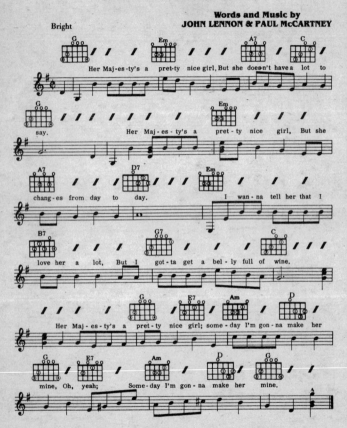

Her Maj-es-ty's a pret-ty nice girl, But she doesn't have a lot to say. Her Maj-es-ty's a pret-ty nice girl, But she chang-es from day to day. I wan-na tell her that I love her a lot, But I got-ta get a bel-ly full of wine. Her Maj-es-ty's a pret-ty nice girl; some-day I'm gon-na make her mine, Oh, yeah; Some-day I'm gon-na make her mine.

Hold Me Tight

Words and Music by
JOHN LENNON & PAUL McCARTNEY

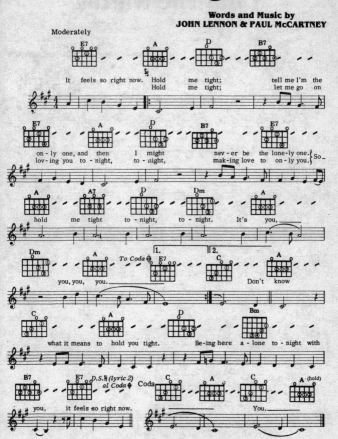

I Am The Walrus

Words and Music by
JOHN LENNON & PAUL McCARTNEY

2. Mr. City Policeman sitting pretty, little policemen in a row.
   See how they fly like Lucy in the sky, see how they run.
   I'm crying.
   Yellow matter custard dripping from a dead dog's eye.
   Crab-a-locker fish-wife pornographic priestess,
   Boy, you been a naughty girl; you let your knickers down.
   I am the eggman, (etc.)
   Sitting in an English garden (etc.)

3. Expert texpert choking smokers; don't you think the joker laughs at you?
   See how they smile like pigs in a sty, see how they snied.
   I'm crying.
   Semolina pilchards climbing up the Eiffel Tower.
   Elementary penguins singing Hare Krishna,
   Man, you should have seen them kicking Edgar Allan Poe.
   I am the eggman, (etc.)

Honey Pie

Words and Music by
JOHN LENNON & PAUL McCARTNEY

I Don't Want
To See You Again

Words and Music by
JOHN LENNON & PAUL McCARTNEY

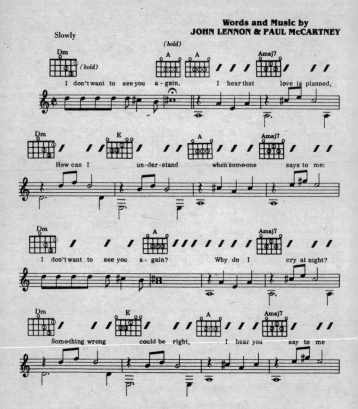

I Need You

Words and Music by
GEORGE HARRISON

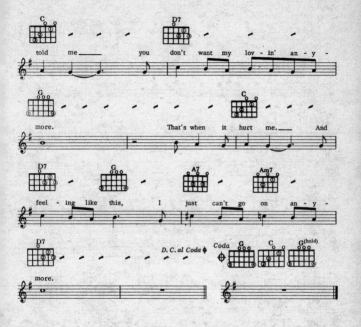

C
told me____ you don't want my lov-in' an-y-

G   C
more.   That's when it hurt me.____ And

D7   G   A7   Am7
feel-ing like this, I just can't go on an-y-

D7   *D. C. al Coda*   Coda G   C   G (hold)
more.

2. Said you had a thing or two to tell me.
   How was I to know you would upset me.
   I didn't realize; as I looked in your eyes
   You told me.
   Oh yes, you told me *(etc.)*

3. Please remember how I feel about you.
   I could never really live without you.
   So come on back and see just what you mean to me.
   I need you.

I Should Have Known Better

Words and Music by
JOHN LENNON & PAUL McCARTNEY

I Will

Words and Music by
JOHN LENNON & PAUL McCARTNEY

Starting note for singing:

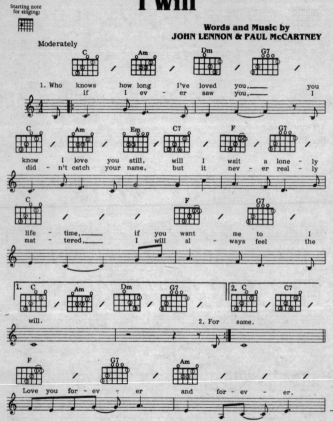

108

love you with all_ my heart; love you when-ev - er we're to-geth-er, love you when we're_ a - part. And when at last I find you,_ your song will fill the air. Sing it loud so I can hear you,_ make it eas-y to be near you_ for the things you do en-dear you to me,_ you know I will.

I'll Be Back

Words and Music by
JOHN LENNON & PAUL McCARTNEY

Moderately

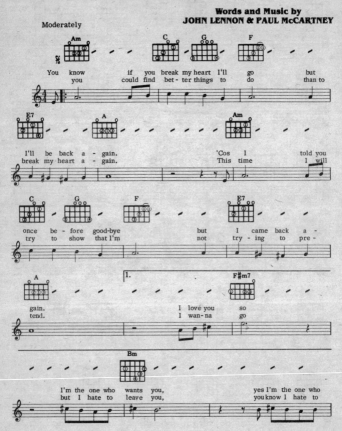

You know if you break my heart I'll go but than to
you could find bet-ter things to do

I'll be back a - gain. 'Cos I told you
break my heart a - gain. This time I will

once be - fore good-bye but I came back a -
try to show that I'm not try - ing to pre -

gain. I love you so
tend. I wan - na go

I'm the one who wants you, yes I'm the one who
but I hate to leave you, you know I hate to

wants you oh ____ ho, oh ____ ho, oh.
leave you oh ____ ho, oh ____

2. I ____ thought that you would re - al - ize ____

that if I ran a - way from you that you would want me too but

I've got a big sur - prise ____ oh ____ ho, oh ____

ho, oh. ho, oh. You, if you break my heart I'll

go but I'll be back a - gain.

111

I'll Cry Instead

Words and Music by
JOHN LENNON & PAUL McCARTNEY

Moderately

I've got ev-'ry reason on earth to be mad,
chip on my shoul-der that's big-ger than my feet,

'Cause I've just lost the on-ly girl I had.
I can't talk to peo-ple that I meet.

If I could get my way, I'd get my-self locked
If I could see you now, I'd try to make you

up to-day, But I can't, so I cry in-stead.
say it some-how, But I can't, so I cry in-stead.

1.   2.

I've got a   Don't want to cry when there's peo-ple

there, I get shy when they start to stare; I'm gon-na hide my-self a-

way - ay, - hay; ___ But I'll come back a - gain some - day. And when I

do you'd bet - ter hide ___ all the girls,

I'm gon - na break their hearts all 'round the world. Yes,

I'm gon - na break them in two, And show you what your lov - in'

man can do, Un-til then I'll cry ___ in - stead. *(hold)*

I'll Get You

Words and Music by
JOHN LENNON & PAUL McCARTNEY

Moderately

Oh yeah, oh yeah, oh yeah, oh yeah. 1. Im-

ag — ine I'm in love with you it's eas — y 'cause I
think a-bout you night and day I need _____ you and it's

know _____ I've im — ag — ined I'm in love with you
true _____ when I think a-bout you I can say, I'm

man — y, man — y, man — y times be — fore. It's not
nev — er, nev — er, nev — er, nev — er blue. So I'm

like me to pre — tend but I'll get you, I'll get you in the
tell — ing you my friend that I'll

Imagine

Starting note for singing:

Slow and steady

Words and Music by
JOHN LENNON

Im-ag-ine there's no heav-en, It's eas-y if you try,

No hell be-low us, A-bove us on-ly sky,

Im-ag-ine all the peo-ple, Liv-ing for to-day, A-ha.

Im-ag-ine there's no coun-tries, It is-n't hard to
Im-ag-ine no pos-ses-sions, I won-der if you

117

I'm A Loser

Words and Music by
JOHN LENNON & PAUL McCARTNEY

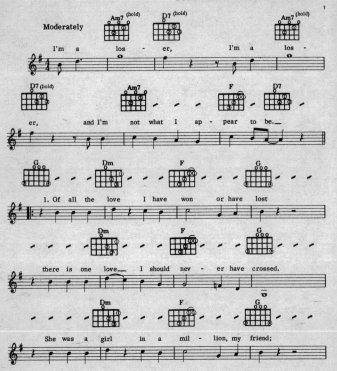

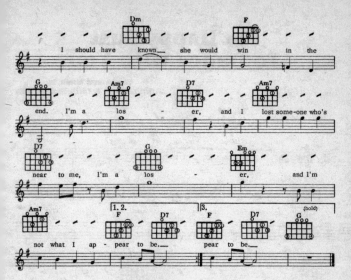

I should have known she would win in the end. I'm a los - er, and I lost some-one who's near to me, I'm a los - er, and I'm not what I ap - pear to be. pear to be.

2. Although I laugh
   And I act like a clown
   Beneath this mask
   I am wearing a frown.

   My tears are falling
   Like rain from the sky
   Is it for her
   Or myself that I cry.

   I'm a loser
   And I lost someone who's near to me
   I'm a loser
   And I'm not what I appear to be.

3. What have I done
   To deserve such a fate
   I realize
   I have left it too late.

   And so it's true
   Pride comes before a fall
   I'm telling you
   So that you won't lose all

   I'm a loser *(etc.)*

I'm Happy Just To Dance With You

Words and Music by
JOHN LENNON & PAUL McCARTNEY

Moderato

I don't wan-na kiss or hold your hand, If it's
I don't need to hug or hold you tight, I just

fun-ny try to un-der-stand, There is
Wan-na dance with you all night, In this

real-ly noth-ing else I'd rath-er do, 'Cause I'm
world there's noth-ing I would rath-er do,

hap-py just to dance with you. Just to dance with you

Is ev-'ry-thing I need. Be-fore this

dance is through I think I'll love you too, I'm so hap-py when you dance with me. If some-bod-y tries to take my place, Let's pre-tend we just can't see his face, In this world there's noth-ing I would rath-er do,_____ 'cause I'm hap-py just to dance with you. Oh, oh, 'cause I'm hap-py just to dance with you. Oh, Oh, Oh, Oh, Oh!

Am   Dm   E7 (No Chord)   F   G   C   G   C   G   F   C   F   G   Am   F   Em   F   G   Am   F   Em   F   G   C

(hold)

If I Needed Someone

Words and Music by
GEORGE HARRISON

Moderately

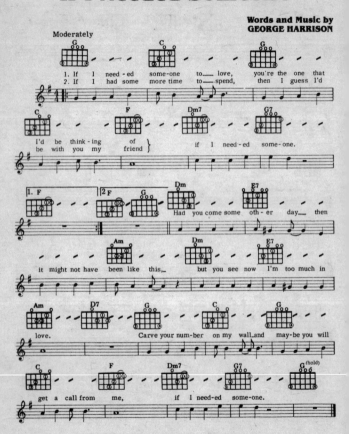

1. If I need-ed some-one to love, you're the one that
2. If I had some more time to spend, then I guess I'd

I'd be think-ing of
be with you my friend } if I need-ed some-one.

Had you come some oth-er day then

it might not have been like this, but you see now I'm too much in

love. Carve your num-ber on my wall and may-be you will

get a call from me, if I need-ed some-one.

I'm Looking Through You

Words and Music by
JOHN LENNON & PAUL McCARTNEY

Moderately

I'm look-ing through you;___ where did you go?
Your lips are mov-ing;___ I can-not hear.

I thought I knew you;___ what did I know?
Your voice is sooth-ing,___ but the words aren't clear.

You don't___ look dif-f'rent, but you have changed;
You don't___ sound dif-f'rent; I've learned the game.

I'm look-ing through you___ you're not___ the same.
I'm look-ing through you___ you're not___ the same.

To Coda

Why, tell me why did you not treat me right?___ Love has a

D. S. al Coda

nas-ty hab-it of dis-ap-pear-ing o-ver-night.

Coda

where.

3. Your thinking of me in the same old way.
You were above me, but not today.
The only difference is you're down there;
I'm looking through you, and you're nowhere.

I'm Only Sleeping

Words and Music by
JOHN LENNON & PAUL McCARTNEY

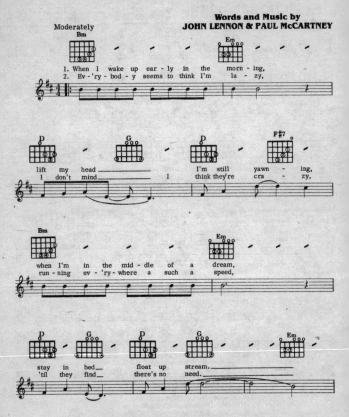

3. Lying there and staring at the ceiling, waiting for a sleepy feeling.
   (Guitar Solo)
   Please don't spoil my day, I'm miles away and after all
   I'm only sleeping.

In My Life

Words and Music by
JOHN LENNON & PAUL McCARTNEY

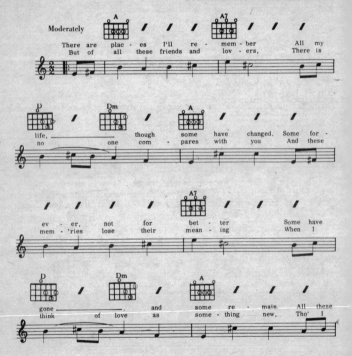

Moderately

There are plac - es I'll re - mem - ber, All my
But of all these friends and lov - ers, There is

life, _____ though some have changed. Some for -
no one com - pares with you And these

ev - er, not for bet - ter Some have
mem - 'ries lose their mean - ing When I

gone _____ and some re - main, All these
think of love as some - thing new, Tho' I

The Inner Light

Words and Music by
GEORGE HARRISON

It's All Too Much

Moderately

Words and Music by
GEORGE HARRISON

2. Floating down the stream of time
From life to life with me.
Makes no difference where you are
Or where you'd like to be.
It's all too much for me to take
The love that's shining all around you.
All the world is birthday cake
So take a piece but not too much.

3. Sail me on a silver sun,
Where I know that I'm free.
Show me that I'm everywhere
And get me home for tea.
It's all too much for me to take
There's plenty there for everybody.
The more you give the more you get
The more it is and it's too much.

Instant Karma!

Words and Music by
JOHN LENNON

Moderately

In - stant Kar - ma's gon - na get you,
In - stant Kar - ma's gon - na get you,

gon - na knock you right on the head! ___
gon - na knock you right in the face! ___

You bet - ter get your - self to - geth - er.
You bet - ter get your - self to - geth - er.

Pret - ty soon you're gon-na be dead!   What in the world you think-ing
Join the hu - man race!   How in the world you gon - na

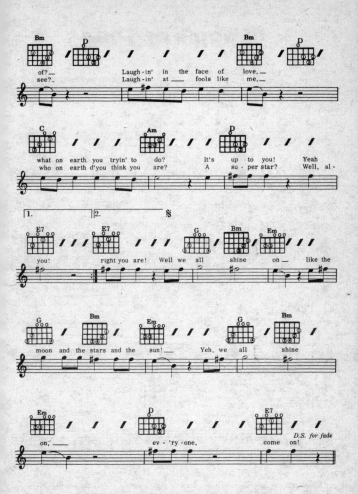

Bm   D

of? _____   Laugh-in' in the face of love, _____
see? _____   Laugh-in' at _____ fools like me, _____

Bm   D

C   Am   D

what on earth you tryin' to   do?   It's   up   to   you!   Yeah
who on earth d'you think you   are?   A   su - per star?   Well, al -

|1.| |2.| %

E7   E7   G   Bm   Em

you!   right you are! Well we all   shine   on _____ like the

G   Bm   Em   G   Bm

moon and the stars and the   sun! _____   Yeh, we   all   shine

Em   D   E7

on, _____   ev - 'ry-one,   come on!   *D.S. for fade*

It Won't Be Long

Words and Music by
JOHN LENNON & PAUL McCARTNEY

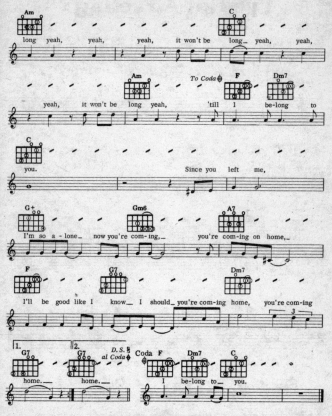

long yeah, yeah, yeah, it won't be long_ yeah, yeah,

yeah, it won't be long yeah, 'till I be-long to

you. Since you left me,

I'm so a-lone_ now you're com-ing, you're com-ing on home,_

I'll be good like I know_ I should_ you're com-ing home, you're com-ing

1. home.__ 2. home.__ Coda I be-long to_ you.

3. Ev'ry day we'll be happy I know,
Now I know that you won't leave me no more,
It won't be long, yeah. (etc.)

I've Got A Feeling

Moderately slow

Words and Music by
JOHN LENNON & PAUL McCARTNEY

Oh please believe me I'd hate to miss the train, oh yeah, oh yeah,
And if you leave me I won't be late again, oh no, oh no, oh no.
Yeah, Yeah, I've got a feeling, yeah!

I've got a feeling that keeps me on my toes, oh yeah, oh yeah.
I've got a feeling, I think that everybody knows, oh yeah, oh yeah, oh yeah.
Yeah, Yeah, I've got a feeling yeah!

I've Just Seen A Face

Words and Music by
JOHN LENNON & PAUL McCARTNEY

1. I've just seen a face, I can't for - get the time or place where we just met, she's just the girl for me and I want all the world to see we've met. Mm mm mm mm mm mm.
2. Had it been an - oth - er day I might have looked the oth - er way and I'd have nev - er been a - ware but as it is I'll dream of her to - night. Da da da da da da.
3. I have nev - er known the like of this I've been a - lone and I have missed things and kept out of sight for oth - er girls were nev - er quite like this. Mm mm mm mm mm mm.

Fall - ing,__ yes I am fall - ing,__ and she keeps call - ing,__ me back a - gain.

gain.

137

Julia

Words and Music by
JOHN LENNON & PAUL McCARTNEY

Slow

D / Bm7 / F#m7 / /

Half of what I say is mean-ing - less,
When I can-not sing my heart,

D / Bm7 / F#m7 / A7 /

But I say it just to reach you Ju - li - a
I can on - ly speak my mind Ju - li - a

D / Bm7 / Am / Am7 / B7 /

1. Ju - li - a, Ju - li - a, O - cean
Ju - li - a, sea - shell - eyes, Wind - y

G9 / Gm7 / *To Coda* D / Bm7 /

child calls me. So I sing a song of love,
smile calls me. So I sing a song of love,

F#m7 / A7 / D / C#m 4 fr. /

Ju - li - a.
Ju - li - a. Her hair of

2. Julia; Sleeping sand,
Silent cloud touch me.
So I sing a song of love for Julia, Julia, Julia.

Lady Madonna

Moderately

Words and Music by
JOHN LENNON & PAUL McCARTNEY

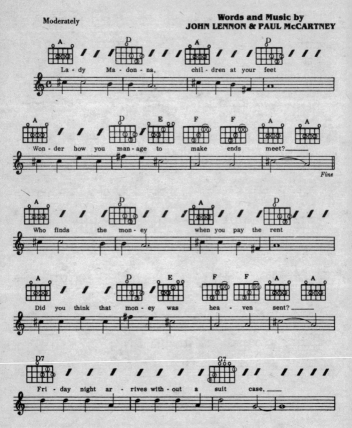

Sun - day morn - ing creep - ing like a nun.

Mon - day's child has learned to tie his shoe - lace.

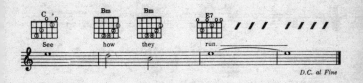

See how they run.

D.C. al Fine

Lady Madonna, baby at your breast,
Wonder how you manage to feed the rest.
Lady Madonna lying on the bed,
Listen to the music playing in your head.

Tuesday afternoon is never ending,
Wednesday morning papers didn't come,
Thursday night your stocking needed mending.
See how they run.

Let It Be

Words and Music by
JOHN LENNON & PAUL McCARTNEY

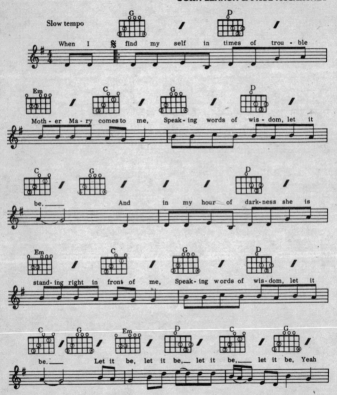

Slow tempo

When I find my self in times of trou - ble

Moth - er Ma - ry comes to me, Speak - ing words of wis - dom, let it

be.___ And in my hour of dark - ness she is

stand - ing right in front of me, Speak - ing words of wis - dom, let it

be.___ Let it be, let it be,___ let it be,___ let it be, Yeah

142

2. And when the broken hearted people
   Living in the world agree,
   There will be an answer, let it be.
   For tho' they may be parted
   There is still a chance that they will see,
   There will be an answer, let it be.
   Let it be, let it be, let it be, let it be,
   Yeah There will be an answer, let it be,
   Let it be, let it be, let it, be, let it be,
   Whisper words of wisdom, let it be.

3. And when the night is cloudy
   There is still a light that shines on me,
   Shine until tomorrow, let it be.
   I wake up to the sound of music
   Mother Mary comes to me,
   Speaking words of wisdom, let it be.
   Let it be, let it be, let it be, let it be,
   Yeah There will be an answer, let it be,
   Let it be, let it be, let it be, let it be,
   Whisper words of wisdom, let it be.

The Long And Winding Road

Words and Music by
JOHN LENNON & PAUL McCARTNEY

Slowly

1. The long and wind-ing road that___ leads to your
2. wild and wind-y night that the rain washed a-

door will nev-er dis-a-pear,
way has left a pool of tears

I've seen that road be-fore, It al-ways
cry-ing for the day, why leave me

leads me here, lead me to your door. The
stand-ing here, let me know the___ way.

Man-y times I've been a-lone and man-y times I've cried,

An-y-way you'll nev-er know the man-y times I've tried but still they lead me

back to the long wind-ing road, You left me stand-ing

here, A long long time a-go Don't leave me

wait-ing here, lead me to your door. Da da da da. (hold)

Love Of The Loved

Words and Music by
JOHN LENNON & PAUL McCARTNEY

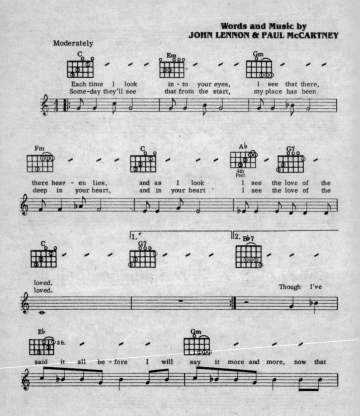

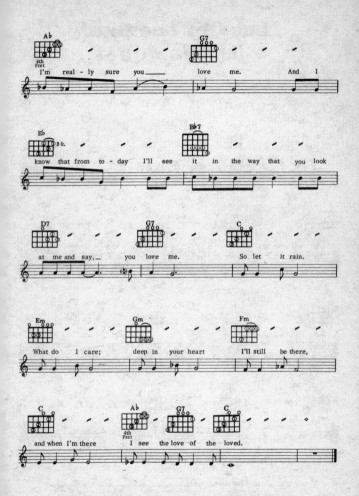

Lucy In The Sky
With Diamonds

Words and Music by
JOHN LENNON & PAUL McCARTNEY

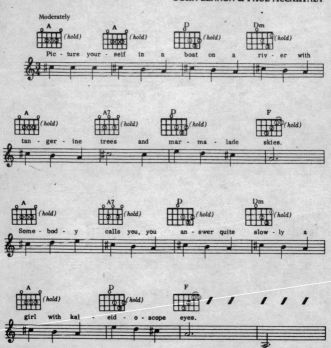

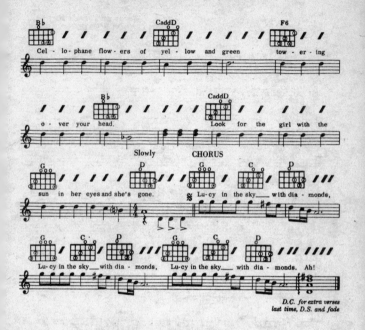

Cel - lo - phane flow - ers of yel - low and green tow - er - ing

o - ver your head. Look for the girl with the

sun in her eyes and she's gone.

Slowly **CHORUS**

Lu - cy in the sky__ with dia - monds,

Lu - cy in the sky__ with dia - monds, Lu - cy in the sky__ with dia - monds. Ah!

D.C. for extra verses
last time, D.S. and fade

Follow her down to a bridge by a fountain
Where rocking horse people eat marshmallow pies.
Ev'ryone smiles as you drift past the flowers
That grow so incredibly high.
Newspaper taxis appear on the shore waiting to take you away
Climb in the back with your head in the clouds and you're gone.

Chorus

Picture yourself on a train in a station
With plasticine porters with looking glass ties.
Suddenly someone is there at the turnstile
The girl with kaleidoscope eyes.

Chorus

Lovely Rita

Words and Music by
JOHN LENNON & PAUL McCARTNEY

1. Lovely Ri-ta, me-ter maid, noth-ing can come be-tween us,
4. Love-ly Ri-ta, me-ter maid, may I in-quire dis-creet-ly,

When it gets dark I tow your heart a-way.
When are you free to take some tea with

2. Stand-ing by a park-ing me-ter, When I caught a glimpse of Ri-ta
3. In a cap she looked much old-er And the bag a-cross her shoul-der

Fill-ing in a tick-et in her lit-tle white book
Made her look a lit-tle like a mil-i-t'ry man.

D.C.
al Coda

me, Love-ly Ri-ta.

(hold)

Took her out and tried to win her, had a laugh and over dinner
Told her I would really like to see her again.
Got the bill and Rita paid it, Took her home and nearly made it
Sitting on a sofa with a sister or two.
Lovely Rita, meter maid, where would I be without you?
Give us a wink and make me think of you, Lovely Rita.

Maggie Mae

**Words and Music by
JOHN LENNON, PAUL McCARTNEY,
GEORGE HARRISON & RICHARD STARKEY**

Magical Mystery Tour

Words and Music by
JOHN LENNON & PAUL McCARTNEY

Moderately

roll up ___ for the mys - te - ry tour.

The ma - gi - cal mys - te - ry tour ___ is
The ma - gi - cal mys - te - ry tour ___ is

wait-ing to take you a - way,
hop-ing to take you a - way,

wait-ing to take you a-
hop-ing to take you a-

1. way.

2. way.

Coda

The ma - gi - cal
The ma - gi - cal

mys - te - ry tour is com-ing to take you a - way,
mys - te - ry tour is dy-ing to take you a - way,

com-ing to take you a - way.
dy-ing to take you a-

way, take you a - way.

Maxwell's Silver Hammer

Words and Music by
JOHN LENNON & PAUL McCARTNEY

Michelle

Words and Music by
JOHN LENNON & PAUL McCARTNEY

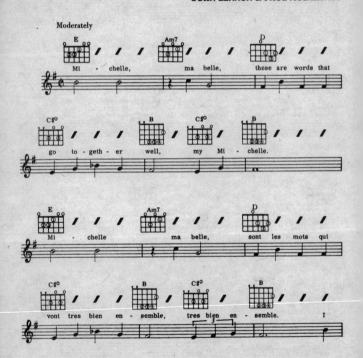

Michelle, ma belle, sont les mots qui vont tres bien ensemble, tres bien ensemble.
I need to, I need to, I need to make you see
Oh, what you mean to me. Until I do I'm hoping you will know what I mean.

I want you, I want you, I want you, I think you know by now
I'll get to you somehow. Until I do, I'm telling you so you'll understand,
My Michelle.

Mother Nature's Son

Words and Music by
JOHN LENNON & PAUL McCARTNEY

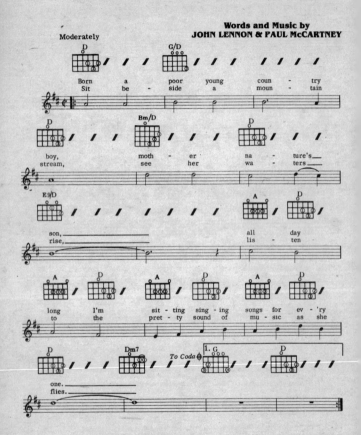

3. Find me in my field of grass,
   Mother nature's son.
   Swaying daisies, sing a lazy song beneath the sun.

The Night Before

Words and Music by
JOHN LENNON & PAUL McCARTNEY

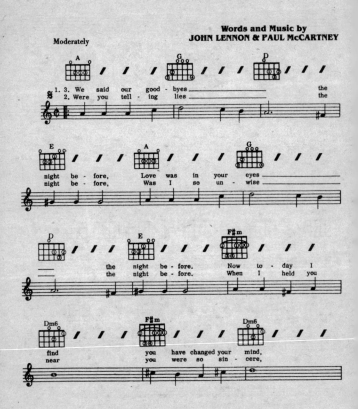

Treat me like you did the night before.

Last night is the night I will re-

mem-ber you by, When I think of

things we did it makes me wan-na cry. *D.S. al Coda*

◆ Coda

Like the night be-fore. (hold)

No Reply

Words and Music by
JOHN LENNON & PAUL McCARTNEY

see man — your in my — face. place. — I tried to tel‑e‑

2.

If I were you I'd re‑al‑ize that

I love you more than an‑y oth‑er

guy. And I'll for‑give the lies that

I heard be‑fore when you

gave me no re‑ply. I tried to tel‑e‑

D.S. ⅓ (2nd verse) al Coda

Coda

No re‑ply, no re‑ply.

Norwegian Wood
(This Bird Has Flown)

Words and Music by
JOHN LENNON & PAUL McCARTNEY

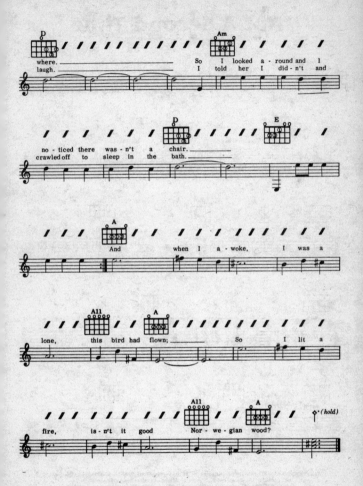

where._____ So I looked a-round and I
laugh._____ I told her I did-n't and

no-ticed there was-n't a chair._____
crawled off to sleep in the bath._____

And when I a-woke, I was a

lone, this bird had flown; _____ So I lit a

fire, is-n't it good Nor-we-gian wood?

Not A Second Time

Words and Music by
JOHN LENNON & PAUL McCARTNEY

Nowhere Man

Words and Music by
JOHN LENNON & PAUL McCARTNEY

Ob-La-Di, Ob-La-Da

Moderately Bright

Words and Music by
JOHN LENNON & PAUL McCARTNEY

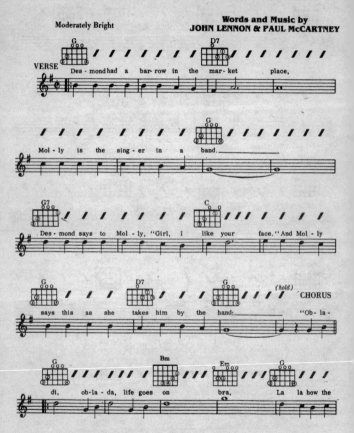

2. Desmond takes a trolley to the jeweller's store,
   Buys a twenty carat golden ring.
   Takes it back to Molly waiting at the door
   And as he gives it to her she begins to sing. (Chorus)

3. Happy ever after in the market place,
   Desmond lets the children lend a hand.
   Molly stays at home and does her pretty face
   And in the evening she still sings it with the band: (Chorus)

Oh! Darling

Words and Music by
JOHN LENNON & PAUL McCARTNEY

Oh! Darling, Please believe me,
I'll never let you down.
Believe me when I tell you,
I'll never do you no harm.

One After 909

Words and Music by
JOHN LENNON & PAUL McCARTNEY

Boogie-rock tempo

My ba - by says she's trav-'ling on the One Af - ter Nine - O - Nine,

I said, move o - ver, hon - ey, I'm travel - ing on that line.

I said move o - ver once, move o - ver twice, Come on ba-by, don't

be cold as ice.__ I said I'm trav-'ling on the One After Nine-O - Nine.

I've got my bag, run to the sta - tion.

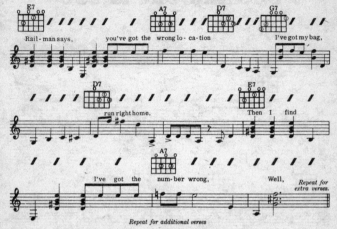

Rail - man says,   you've got the wrong lo - ca - tion   I've got my bag,

run right home.   Then I find

I've got the num - ber wrong,   Well,   *Repeat for extra verses.*

Repeat for additional verses

2. I begged her not to go and I begged her on my bended knees,
   You're only fooling around, you're only fooling around with me.
   I said move over once, move over twice,
   Come on, baby, don't be cold as ice.
   I said I'm trav'ling on the One After Nine-O-Nine.

3. Repeat first verse.

Coda   I said we're trav - 'ling on the   One Af - ter Nine O,   2

I said we're trav'ling on the One Af - ter Nine - O - Nine.

One And One Is Two

Moderately

Words and Music by
JOHN LENNON & PAUL McCARTNEY

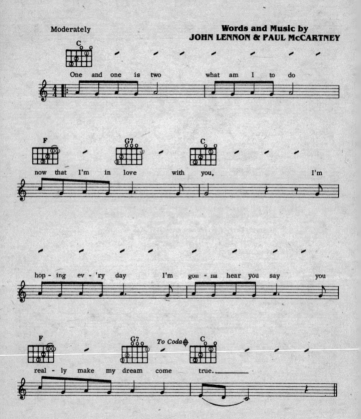

One and one is two what am I to do now that I'm in love with you, I'm hop-ing ev-'ry day I'm gon-na hear you say you real-ly make my dream come true.

To Coda

3. If you say that you're gonna be mine,
   Everything's alright.
   All the world would look so fine
   If you'd be mine tonight.

Oo You

Words and Music by
PAUL McCARTNEY

1. Look like a wom - an
2. Walk like a wom - an

Dressed like a la - dy
Sing like a black-bird

Talk like a ba - by
Eat like a hun - gry

3. Look like a woman,
Dressed like a lady,
Talk like a baby,
Love like a woman.

Paperback Writer

Words and Music by
JOHN LENNON & PAUL McCARTNEY

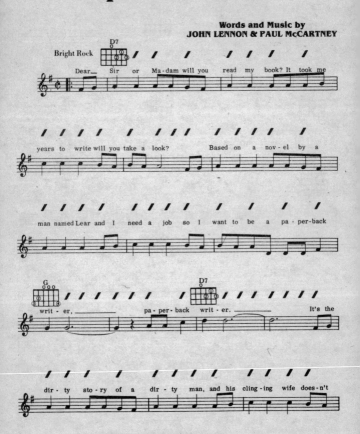

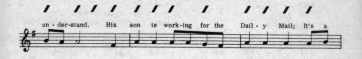

un-der-stand. His son is work-ing for the Dail - y Mail; It's a

stead - y job, but he wants to be a pa - per - back

G

D7

writ - er,_____ pa - per-back writ - er._____

It's a thousand pages, give or take a few,
I'll be writing more in a week or two.
I can make it longer if you like the style,
I can change it 'round and I want to be a paperback writer, paperback writer.
If you really like it you can have the rights,
It could make a million for you overnight.
If you must return it you can send it here;
But I need a break and I want to be a paperback writer, paperback writer

D7 (hold) D7 (hold) D7

pa - per-back writ - er.

Repeat and Fade

Penny Lane

Words and Music by
JOHN LENNON & PAUL McCARTNEY

Moderately Bright

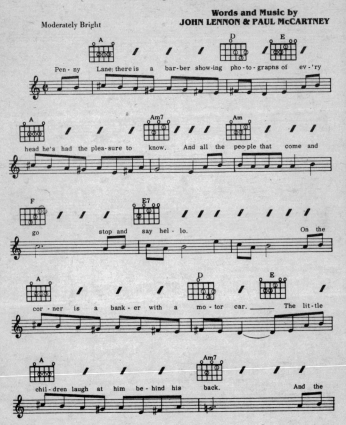

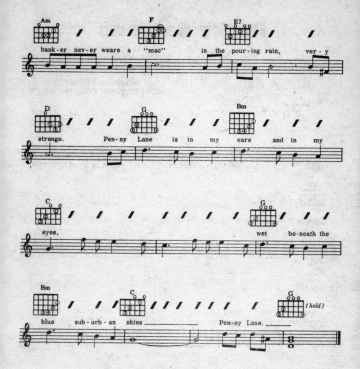

Back in Penny Lane: there is a fireman with an hourglass.
And in his pocket is a portrait of the queen.
He likes to keep his fire engine clean, it's a clean machine.
Penny Lane is in my ears and in my eyes.
Full of fish and finger pies in summer meanwhile

Back behind the shelter in the middle of the round-a-bout
A pretty nurse is selling poppies from a tray.
And tho' she feels as if she's in a play she is anyway.
Back in Penny Lane: the barber shaves another customer.
We see the banker sitting waiting for a trim.
And the the fireman rushes in from the pouring rain, very strange.

Rocky Raccoon

Brightly, in 2 (♩=1 beat)

Words and Music by
JOHN LENNON & PAUL McCARTNEY

(Spoken) Now somewhere in the Black Mountain Hills of Dakota, there lived a
He said, "I'm going to get that boy."

young boy named Rocky Raccoon. And one day his woman
So one day he walked into

ran off with another guy; Hit Rocky in the eye; Rocky didn't like that.
town and booked himself a room in a local saloon.

Am7

Rock - y Rac - coon___ checked in - to his room___
she and her man___ who called him - self Dan___ were

D7

G7   C   C/B

on - ly to find___ Gid-eon's Bi - ble.
in the next room___ at the hoe - down.

Am7

Rock - y had come___ e - quipped with a gun___ to
Rock - y burst in___ and grin - ning a grin,___ He said,

D7

G7   C   C/B

shoot off the legs___ of his ri - val. His
"Dan - ny boy, this___ is a show - down." But

Am7   D7

ri - val it seems___ had bro - ken his dreams___ by
Dan - iel was hot,   he drew first and shot___ and

G7   C   C/B

steal - ing the girl___ of his fan - cy. Her
Rock - y col - lapsed___ in the cor - ner. *(continue as guitar solo)*

185

Am7

"Rock-y, you met_ your match," And Rock-y said, "Doc, it's on-ly a
Gid - eon checked out___ And he_ left it no doubt

D7

scratch, And I'll be bet-ter, I'll be bet-ter Doc, as soon_ as I'm
To help with good Rock_ y's re - vi -

G7

1. C   C/B   2. C   C/B

a - ble."   Now - val.

Am7   D7

G7

1. C   C/B   2. C

187

Run For Your Life

Words and Music by
JOHN LENNON & PAUL McCARTNEY

Medium beat

Verse

1. Well I'd rath-er see you dead, lit-tle girl, than to
know that I'm a wick-ed guy and I was

be with an-oth-er man.   You'd bet-ter keep your
born with a jeal-ous mind.   And I can't spend my

head, lit-tle girl, or I won't know where I
whole life try-in' just to make you toe the

Chorus

am.
line.   You'd bet-ter run for your life if you

D7   can, lit - tle girl.   **Am7**   Hide your head in the

D7   sand, lit - tle girl.   **Am**   Catch you with an - oth - er

F   **E7**   **Am**   man that's the end, ah, lit - tle girl.

C7

(Guitar)

1. 2. 3. **C7**   **4** **C7**   *Repeat and fade*

2. Well, you   No no no.   No no

3. Let this be a sermon.
   I mean everything I said.
   Baby, I'm determined,
   And I'd rather see you dead.

   Chorus

4. I'd rather see you dead, little girl,
   Than to be with another man.
   You'd better keep your head, little girl,
   Or I won't know where I am.

   Chorus

189

Sgt. Pepper's
Lonely Hearts Club Band

Starting note for singing:

Moderately bright

Words and Music by
JOHN LENNON & PAUL McCARTNEY

It was twen-ty years a-go to-day Ser-geant
I don't real-ly want to stop the show but I

Pep-per taught the band to play. They've been go-ing in and out of
thought you might like to know That the sing-er's gon-na sing a

style, but they're guar-an-teed to raise a smile. So
song, and he wants you all to sing a - long. So

may I in-tro-duce to you the act you've known for all these
let me in-tro-duce to you the one and on-ly Bil-ly

years. Ser-geant Pep-per's Lone - ly Hearts Club Band.
Shears.

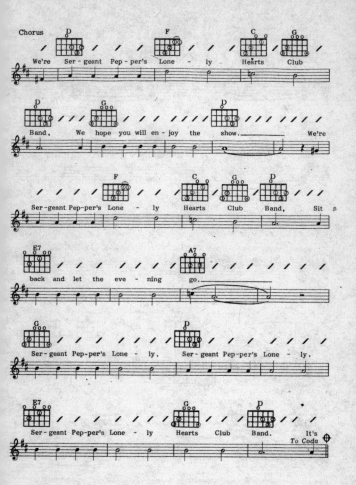

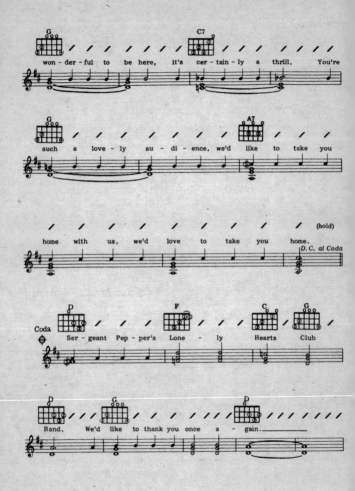

192

Sexy Sadie

Words and Music by
JOHN LENNON & PAUL McCARTNEY

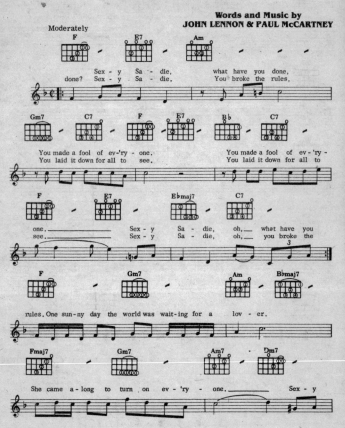

She Said She Said

Words and Music by
JOHN LENNON & PAUL McCARTNEY

Moderately

1. She said _____ I know what it's like to be dead,
2. I said _____ who put all those things in your hair,

I know what it is to be sad.
Things that make me feel that I'm mad.

And she's
And you're

mak-ing me feel like I've nev-er been born. *Guitar*

1. 2.

She said you don't un-der-

stand what I said, I said; No, no, no, you're wrong, when I was a

Polythene Pam

Words and Music by
JOHN LENNON & PAUL McCARTNEY

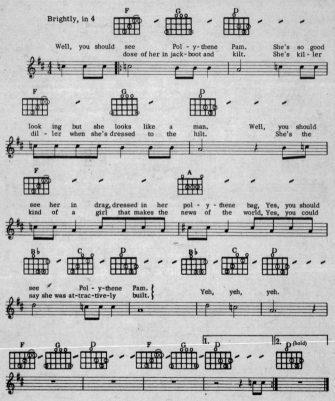

Brightly, in 4

Well, you should see Pol-y-thene Pam. She's so good
dose of her in jack-boot and kilt. She's kil-ler

look ing but she looks like a man. Well, you should
dil - ler when she's dressed to the hilt. She's the

see her in drag, dressed in her pol - y - thene bag, Yes, you should
kind of a girl that makes the news of the world, Yes, you could

see Pol - y - thene Pam.
say she was at-trac-tive-ly built. Yeh, yeh, yeh.

1. 2. (hold)

Strawberry Fields Forever

**Words and Music by
JOHN LENNON & PAUL McCARTNEY**

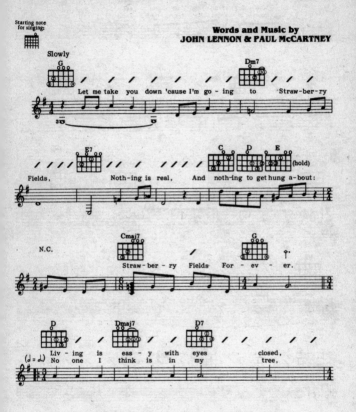

Mis - un - der - stand - ing all you see.
I mean it must be high or low.

It's get - ting hard to be some - one, but it all __ works out;
That is, you know you can't tune in, but it's all _____ right,

it does - n't mat - ter much to me.
that is, I think it's not too bad.

(hold) (hold)

Let me take you down 'cause I'm go - ing

to Straw - ber - ry Fields,   Noth - ing is

200

Taxman

Words and Music by
GEORGE HARRISON

Medium Rock

1. Let me tell you how it will be;
five per-cent ap-pear too small,

There's one for you, nine-teen for me.
Be thank-ful I don't take it all.

'Cause I'm the tax-man,

Last time to Coda

Yeh, I'm the tax-man. Should 2. Should
4. Now

tax-man. If you drive a car I'll

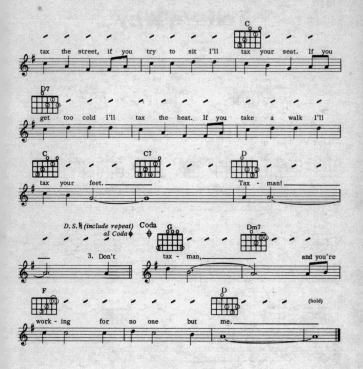

3. Don't ask me what I want it for,
   If you don't want to pay some more.
   'Cause I'm the taxman,
   Yeh, I'm the taxman.

4. Now my advice for those who die:
   Beware the pennies on your eye!
   'Cause I'm the taxman,
   Yeh, I'm the taxman,
   And you're working for no one but me.

Tell Me Why

Words and Music by
JOHN LENNON & PAUL McCARTNEY

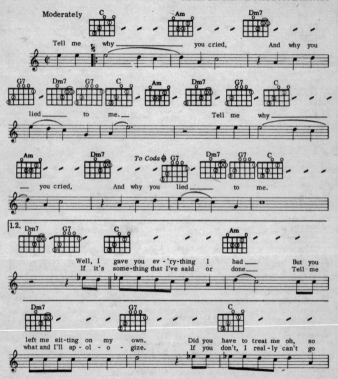

Moderately

Tell me why __ you cried, And why you lied __ to me. __ Tell me why __ you cried, And why you lied __ to me.

To Coda

1.2.

Well, I gave you ev-'ry-thing I had __ But you left me sit-ting on my own.
If it's some-thing that I've said or done __ Tell me what and I'll ap-ol-o-gize.

Did you have to treat me oh, so
If you don't, I real-ly can't go

bad?___ All I do is hang my head and moan.
on ___ Hold-ing back these tears in my eyes. } Tell me

3 Well, I beg you on my bend-ed knees,___ If you'll

on-ly lis-ten to my pleas, Is there an-y-thing I can

do?___ 'Cause I real-ly can't stand it, I'm so in love with___

you. Tell me lied___ to___

me.

D.S. al Coda

Coda

4th Fret

(bold)

205

Things We Said Today

Words and Music by
JOHN LENNON & PAUL McCARTNEY

You say you will love me if I have to go,
You'll be think-ing of me some-how I will know.

You say you'll be mine girl 'til the end of time,
These days such a kind me girl seems so hard to find.

Some-day when I'm lone-ly, wish-ing you were'nt so far a-way,
Some-day when we're dream-ing, deep in love not a lot to say,

Then I will re-mem-ber Things we said to-day.
Then we will re-mem-ber Things we said to-

day. Me, I'm just the luck-y kind, love to hear you

Think For Yourself

Words and Music by
GEORGE HARRISON

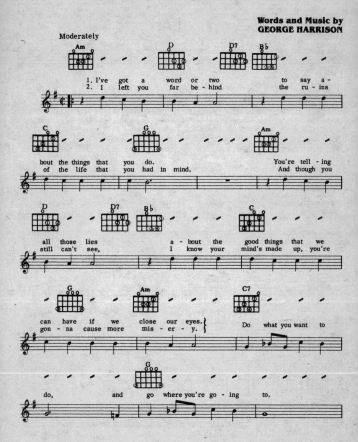

208

3. Although your mind's opaque
   Try thinking more if just for your own sake.
   The future still looks good
   And you've got time to rectify all the things that you should.

This Boy
(Ringo's Theme)

Words and Music by
JOHN LENNON & PAUL McCARTNEY

Ticket To Ride

Words and Music by
JOHN LENNON & PAUL McCARTNEY

D

care.	2. She
1.	2.

G7

don't know why she's rid-ing so high____ She ought-ta

think twice, she ought-ta do right by me. Be-

A

G7

fore she gets to say-ing good-bye,____ She ought-ta

A

think twice, she ought-ta do right by me.

D.C. al Coda

A7sus4   D

Coda

ride, but she don't care,   My ba-by don't care.

(hold)

Repeat and fade

Tip Of My Tongue

Words and Music by
JOHN LENNON & PAUL McCARTNEY

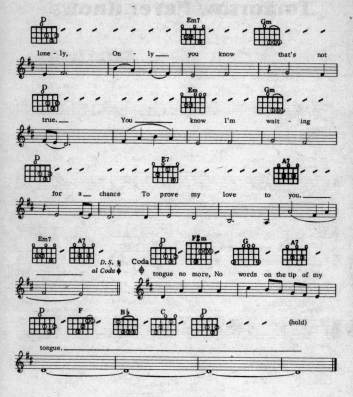

3. Soon enough my time will come,
And after all is said and done
I'll marry you and we will live as one,
With no more words on the tip of my tongue no more,
No words on the tip of my tongue.

Tomorrow Never Knows

Words and Music by
JOHN LENNON & PAUL McCARTNEY

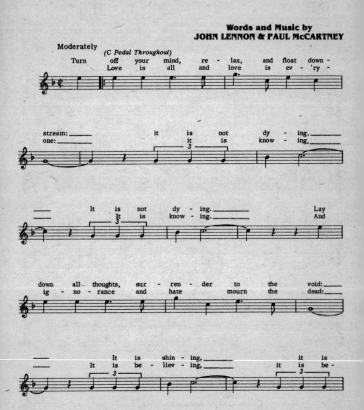

Tell Me What You See

Words and Music by
JOHN LENNON & PAUL McCARTNEY

Moderately

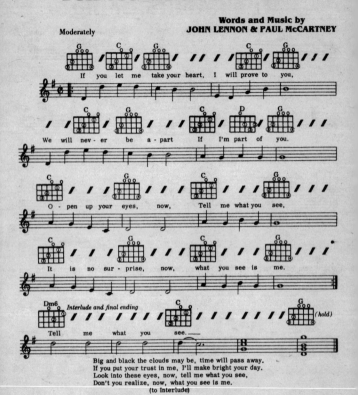

If you let me take your heart, I will prove to you,

We will nev-er be a-part If I'm part of you.

O-pen up your eyes, now, Tell me what you see,

It is no sur-prise, now, what you see is me.

Interlude and final ending

Tell me what you see. _____ (hold)

Big and black the clouds may be, time will pass away.
If you put your trust in me, I'll make bright your day.
Look into these eyes, now, tell me what you see,
Don't you realize, now, what you see is me.
(to Interlude)

Listen to me one more time, how can I get through?
Can't you try to see that I'm tryin' to get to you?
Open up your eyes, now, tell me what you see.
It is no surprise now, what you see is me.
(to Final Ending)

What You're Doing

Words and Music by
JOHN LENNON & PAUL McCARTNEY

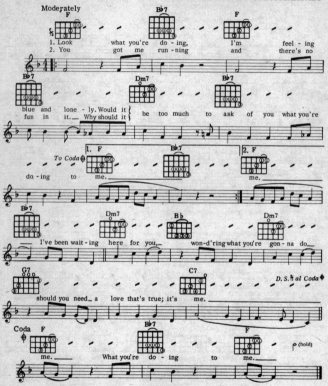

We Can Work It Out

Words and Music by
JOHN LENNON & PAUL McCARTNEY

Moderately Slow

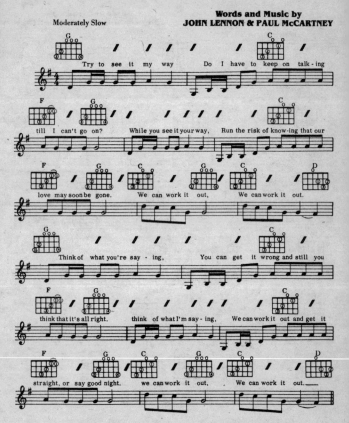

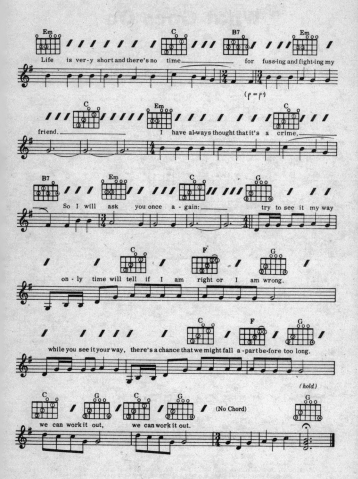

We Can Work It Out

Em   C   B7   Em
Life is ver-y short and there's no time____   for fuss-ing and fight-ing my

(♩ = ♩)

C   Em   C
friend.____   I have al-ways thought that it's a crime,____

B7   Em   C   G
So I will ask   you once a-gain:____   try to see it my way

C   F   G
on-ly time will tell if I am right or I am wrong.

C   F   G
while you see it your way, there's a chance that we might fall a-part be-fore too long.

(hold)

C   G   C   G   (No Chord)   G
we can work it out,   we can work it out.

221

What Goes On

Words and Music by
**JOHN LENNON, PAUL McCARTNEY,
& RICHARD STARKEY**

Moderately

What goes on in your heart, What goes on in your mind? You are tear - ing me a - part When you treat me so un - kind. What goes on in your mind? 1. The

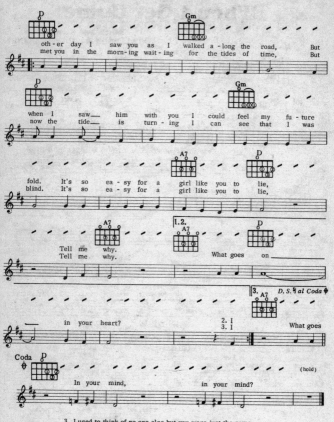

oth-er day I saw you as I walked a-long the road, But
met you in the morn-ing wait-ing for the tides of time, But

when I saw___ him with you I could feel my fu-ture
now the tide___ is turn-ing I can see that I was

fold. It's so ea-sy for a girl like you to lie,
blind. It's so ea-sy for a girl like you to lie,

Tell me why.
Tell me why.   What goes on

in your heart?   What goes

Coda
In your mind,   in your mind?   (hold)

3. I used to think of no one else but you were just the same,
   You didn't even think of me as someone with a name.
   Did you mean to break my heart and watch me die,
   Tell me why.
   What goes on in your heart, *(etc.)*

When I Get Home

Words and Music by
JOHN LENNON & PAUL McCARTNEY

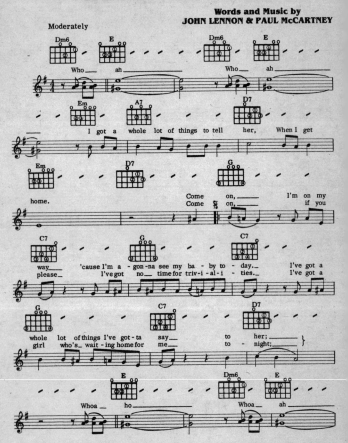

3. Come on, let me through.
I've got so many things I've got to do.
I've got no bus'ness being here with you this way;
Whoa ho, Whoa ah (etc.)

225

With A Little Help From My Friends

Words and Music by
JOHN LENNON & PAUL McCARTNEY

Moderately

1. What would you do if I sang out of tune, would you
2. What do I do when my love is a - way, does it
3. Would you be - lieve in a love at first sight? Yes, I'm

stand up and walk out on me? Lend me your ears and I'll
wor - ry you to be a - lone? How do I feel by the
certain that it happens all the time. What do you see when you

sing you a song and I'll try not to sing out of key, Oh I get
end of the day are you sad be - cause you're on your own? No, I get
turn out the light? I can't tell you but I know it's mine. Oh, I get

by with a lit - tle help from my friends.
by with a lit - tle help from my friends.
by with a lit - tle help from my friends. Mm. I get

high with a lit‑tle help from my friends Mm. I'm gon‑na

try with a lit‑tle help from my friends. **1.** friends. **2.** *To next strain* Do you

3. *Fine* friends. need an‑y‑bod‑y? I

need some‑bod‑y to love. Could it be an‑y‑

bod‑y? I want some‑bod‑y to love. *D.C. al Fine*

Within You Without You

Words and Music by
GEORGE HARRISON

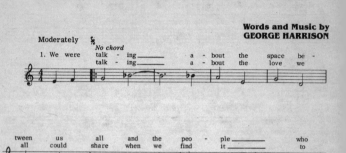

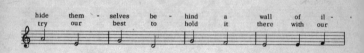

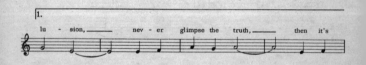

2. 3.
love, with our love___ we could save the world.___
know, they can't see.___ Are you one of them?___

If they on-ly knew. _____
Guitar _____ }   *Gtr.*

{ Try to re-a-lize it's all with-
{ When you've seen be-yond your-self then

in your-self, no one else can make you change.___
you may find, peace of mind is wait-ing there.___

And to see you're real-ly on-ly ver-y small and
And the time will come when you see we're all one and

To Coda ⊕

life flows on with-in you and with-out you.___ *D.S.* ⅜ *al Coda* ⊕
(hold)   3. We were

Coda ⊕
life flows on with-in you and with-out you.
(hold)   *(hold) Gtr.*

3. We were talking, about the love that's gone so cold
   And the people, who gain the world and lose their soul
   They don't know, they can't see,
   Are you one of them?

The Word

Words and Music by
JOHN LENNON & PAUL McCARTNEY

Say the word and you'll be free, Say the word and be like me. Say the word I'm think-ing of Have you heard the word is love? It's so fine, it's sun-shine, It's the word

3. Say the word and you'll be free,
   Say the word and be like me.
   Say the word I'm thinking of.
   Have you heard the word is love?
   It's so fine, it's sunshine,
   It's the word love.
   Now that I know what I feel must be right,
   I mean to show ev'rybody the light.

4. Give the word a chance to say
   That the word is just the way.
   It's the word I'm thinking of
   And the only word is love.
   It's so fine, it's sunshine,
   It's the word love.
   Say the word love. Say the word love.

231

World Without Love

Words and Music by
JOHN LENNON & PAUL McCARTNEY

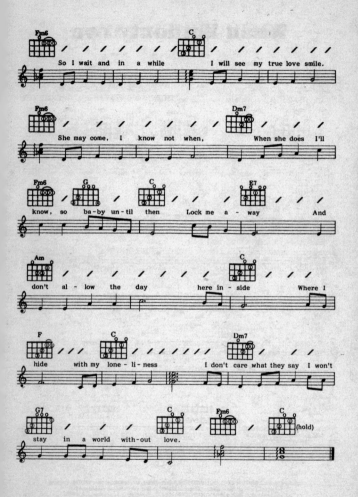

So I wait and in a while I will see my true love smile.

She may come, I know not when, When she does I'll

know, so ba-by un-til then Lock me a-way And

don't al-low the day here in-side Where I

hide with my lone-li-ness I don't care what they say I won't

stay in a world with-out love.

(hold)

When I'm Sixty Four

Words and Music by
JOHN LENNON & PAUL McCARTNEY

Starting note for singing:

Moderately, with a lilt; play ♩♩♩ as ♩♩♩

When I get old - er, los-ing my hair   man - y   years from
I could be hand - y   mend-ing a fuse   when your lights have

now,   Will you still be send-ing me   a   val - en - tine,
gone,   You can knit a sweat-er by the fire - side,

birth - day greet - ings   bot - tle of wine?   If I'd been out   till
Sun - day morn - ing   go   for a   ride.   Do - ing the gar - den,

quar - ter to   three,   would you   lock   the   door?
dig - ging the   weeds   who could   ask   for   more?

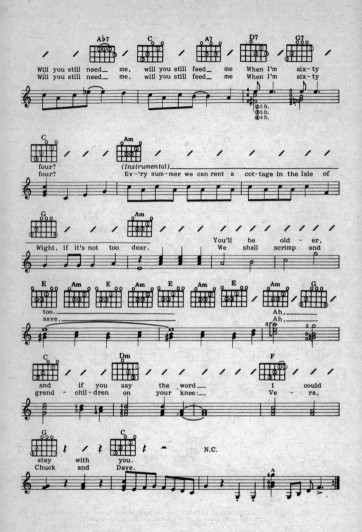

Will you still need me, will you still feed me When I'm six-ty
Will you still need me, will you still feed me When I'm six-ty

four?
four? *(Instrumental)* Ev-'ry sum-mer we can rent a cot-tage in the Isle of

Wight, if it's not too dear. You'll be old-er, We shall scrimp and

too.
save, Ah, Ah,

and if you say the word I could
grand-chil-dren on your knee: Ve-ra,

stay with you.
Chuck and Dave.

N.C.

Your Mother Should Know

Words and Music by
JOHN LENNON & PAUL McCARTNEY

Yellow Submarine

Words and Music by
JOHN LENNON & PAUL McCARTNEY

So we sailed up to the sun,
Till we found the sea of green,
And we lived beneath the waves,
In our Yellow Submarine. (Cho.)

And our friends are all aboard,
Many more of them live next door,
And the band begins to play. (Inst.)
(Chorus)

As we live a life of ease,
Everyone of us has all we need,
Sky of blue and sea of green,
In our Yellow Submarine. (Cho.)

Yer Blues

Words and Music by
JOHN LENNON & PAUL McCARTNEY

3. The black cloud crossed my mind,
Blue mist 'round my soul.
I feel so suicidal,
Even hate my rock and roll.

Yes It Is

Words and Music by
JOHN LENNON & PAUL McCARTNEY

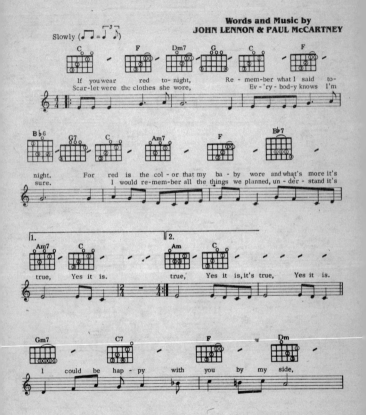

Slowly

If you wear red to-night,
Re-mem-ber what I said to-night.
Scar-let were the clothes she wore,
Ev-'ry-bod-y knows I'm sure.

For red is the col-or that my ba-by wore and what's more it's true, Yes it is.
I would re-mem-ber all the things we planned, un-der-stand it's true, Yes it is, it's true, Yes it is.

I could be hap-py with you by my side,

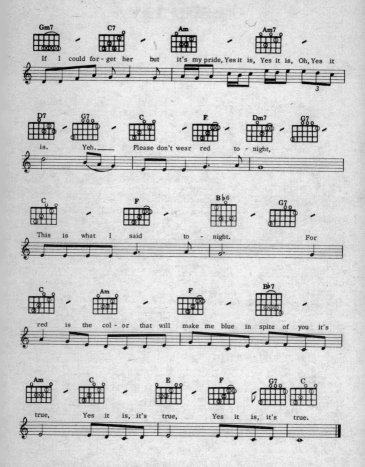

243

Yesterday

Words and Music by
JOHN LENNON & PAUL McCARTNEY

You Like Me Too Much

Words and Music by
GEORGE HARRISON

Moderately

1. Though you're gone a - way this morn - ing, you'll be
   tried be - fore to leave me but you

back a - gain to - night, tell - ing me there'll be no
have - n't got the nerve to walk out and make me

next time if I just don't treat you right. You'll
lone - ly which is all that I de - serve. You'll

nev - er leave me and you know it's true,
nev - er leave me and you know it's true, true,

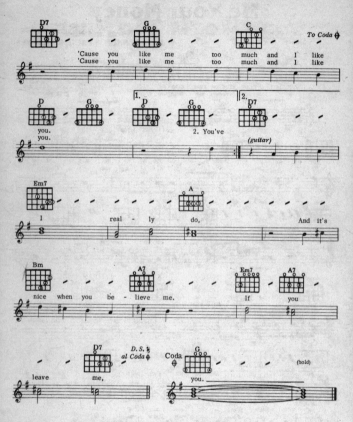

D7 **G** **C** To Coda ⊕

'Cause you like me too much and I like
'Cause you like me too much and I like

D **G** **1. D** **G** **2. D7**

you.
you.   2. You've   (guitar)

Em7 **A**

I   real - ly   do,   And it's

Bm **A7** **Em7** **A7**

nice when you be - lieve me.   If   you

D7 D. S. % Coda ⊕ **G**
al Coda ⊕

leave   me,   you.   (hold)

3. I will follow you and bring you back where you belong
   'Cause I couldn't really stand it, I admit that I was wrong,
   I wouldn't let you leave me 'cause it's true,
   'Cause you like me too much and I like you.

You Never Give Me Your Money

Words and Music by
JOHN LENNON & PAUL McCARTNEY

Slowly

1. You nev-er give me your mon-ey, you on-ly give me your
2. I nev-er give you my num-ber, I on-ly give you my

fun-ny pa-per. And in the mid-dle of ne-go-ti-a-tions you
sit-u-a-tion. And in the mid-dle of in-vest-ig-a-tion I

break down. Out of col-lege, mon-ey spent,
break down. 1. 2. An-y job-ber got the sack,

see no fu-ture, pay no rent, All the mon-ey's gone, no-where to
Mon-day morn-ing turn-ing back yel-low lor-ry slow no-where to

3. go. 4. go. But oh, that ma-gic feel-ing: no-where to

go. Oh, that ma-gic feel-ing no-where to

You Won't See Me

Words and Music by
JOHN LENNON & PAUL McCARTNEY

Medium Rock beat

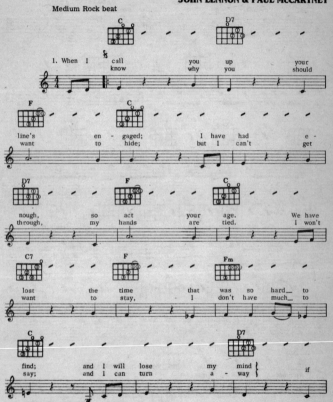

1. When I call know / you / up / your
why you should

line's en- gaged; I have had e-
want to hide; but I can't get

nough, so act your age. We have
through, my hands are tied. I won't

lost the time that was so hard to
want to stay, I don't have much to

find; and I will lose my mind
say; and I can turn a - way } if

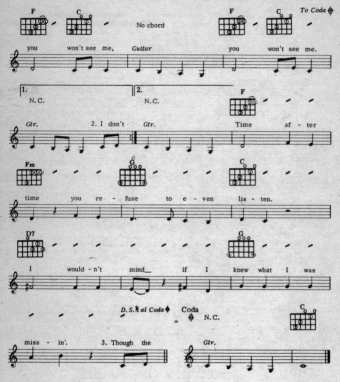

F   C   No chord   F   C   To Coda

you won't see me, *Guitar*   you won't see me.

1.
N.C.
2.
N.C.
F

Gtr.   2. I don't *Gtr.*   Time   af - ter

Fm   G   C

time   you re - fuse to e - ven lis - ten.

D7   G

I   would -n't   mind___   if I   knew what I   was

D. S. ⅗ al Coda   Coda
N.C.
C

miss - in'.   3. Though the   *Gtr.*

3. Though the days are few, they're filled with tears;
   And since I lost you, it feels like years.
   Yes, it seems so long since you've been gone;
   And I just can't go on
   If you won't see me, you won't see me.

You're Going To Lose That Girl

Words and Music by
JOHN LENNON & PAUL McCARTNEY

You've Got To Hide Your Love Away

Words and Music by
JOHN LENNON & PAUL McCARTNEY

Starting note
for singing:

Fast, in 6 (each ♪ = 1 beat)

Here I stand with head in hand, turn my face to the
How can I e - ven try? I can nev - er

wall. If she's gone I can't go on
win. Hear - ing them, see - ing them

feel - ing two foot small.
in the state I'm in.

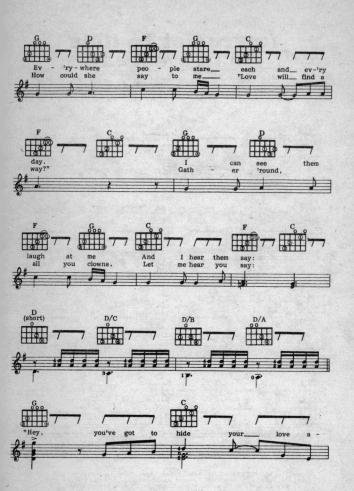

Ev - 'ry - where peo - ple stare___ each and ev-'ry
How could she say to me___ "Love will__ find a

day. I can see them
way?" Gath - er 'round,

laugh at me all you clowns, And I hear them say:
all you clowns, Let me hear you say:

"Hey, you've got to hide your___ love a -

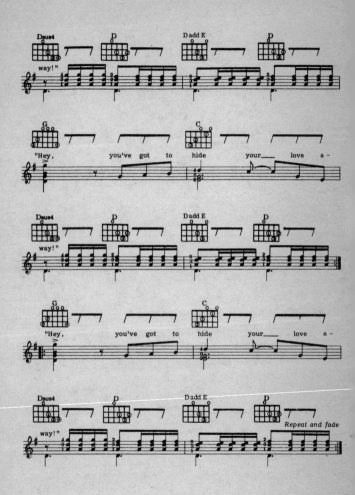